Message from the Dog…Learning From Great Humans

By Miss Zooey & Cindy Bertram

ISBN: 9798530767708

Photo Credits:

Photo of Sister Jean Dolores Schmidt, Chaplain, Loyola Ramblers courtesy of Loyola University Chicago
Photo of Sister Jean Dolores Schmidt with Cindy Bertram taken by Cindy Bertram
Photo of Captain Kate McCue courtesy of Celebrity Cruises®
Photo of Richard E. Sasso, Chairman of MSC Cruises® USA Courtesy of MSC Cruises®
Photo of Herbert Kelleher, Southwest Airlines Co. courtesy of Southwest Airlines Co.
Photos of Ruth taken by Cindy Bertram
Photo of Patricia Rickard taken by Cindy Bertram
Photo of Rudi Schreiner, President & Co-Founder of AmaWaterways™ courtesy of AmaWaterways™
Photos of Nicholas Rago, President & CEO, Consultants to Management provided by Nicholas Rago

Photo of Cindy Bertram taken by Dennis Crane

Photos of Miss Zooey taken by Cindy Bertram
Additional Photos in this book were taken by Cindy Bertram

NOTE:

AmaWaterways™ is a registered trademark of
AmaWaterways™ and used with permission.
Celebrity Cruises® is a registered trademark of Celebrity
Cruises® and used with permission.
MSC Cruises® is a registered trademark of MSC Mediterranean
Shipping Company Holdings SA

Southwest Airlines Co. gave permission for use of Herbert
Kelleher's letter to Cindy Bertram

A special thank-you to Terry Lopez for his help designing the
jacket cover for my book.

Contents

Dedication

As a smart young lady who walks on the floor with 4 legs instead of two, Miss Zooey is also a great listener, who is always open to learning new things. We do tend to talk quite a bit, and as a result? We came up with the idea for this book.

Miss Zooey actually had to relocate herself from Florida to the Midwest and has wonderful parents. She has adjusted extremely well, and enjoys frolicking in the snow, as well as running in the back yard. She has a bit of a protective nature as well. Miss Zooey is open to learning new things, is a great listener, and in our chats, Miss Zooey provides her own great insights.

 Miss Zooey and I are both fascinated by sharing insights, stories that share positive things, and great leaders.

Fascinated by great people and great leaders, Miss Zooey loves hearing about ones I have been honored to know and interact with. And we both agree that the best leaders and people are ones who willing to share their time and expertise.

So, we are dedicating this book to a few people. As far as Miss Zooey, she wants to dedicate this to her human mom and dad, Jodee and Bob, who adopted her.

For me, I have a few people who have inspired me. These include Sister Jean Dolores Schmidt, Chaplain for the Loyola University Chicago Rambler's Basketball team. In her role as Chaplain, she cheered the Loyola Ramblers on in diverse ways through their journey to being in the Final Four in spring 2018. Known as Sister Jean, she has also spent her life inspiring and mentoring both young men and women in her roles, first teaching and then as Chaplain.

Another is Richard "Rick" Sasso, Chairman, MSC Cruises® USA. I have been fortunate to know Rick for several years, thanks to my diverse work in and writing about the cruise industry. Rick has always been a personal hero, a long-distance mentor, and friend. Miss Zooey likes the fact that he calls me his "pen pal." Rick has always encouraged me and has told me during tough times, "Cindy, NEVER EVER give up!"

Rick also encouraged me to write my very first book, and as a result of getting that one written and published late 2018 I decided it was time for me to write another book, utilizing Miss Zooey's wonderful inspiration, thanks to our talks.

INTRODUCTION

When Cindy and I (by the way, I am Miss Zooey) first decided we needed to write this book, we knew it was important to continue learning and growing via diverse ways. We both went to school. Yes, I took obedience training lessons myself, and Cindy studied and got 2 degrees from two different universities. She is a proud Loyola girl and did her Masters' Degree in Business Administration from Loyola University Chicago.

School learning was good, but as Cindy and I both realized, the world continues to change, whether you walk on four legs (like me) or two legs (like Cindy.)

It is important to continue learning and be open to a walking (or running) on a new path. The best way is to learn from other humans, including leaders. Cindy and I do that.

Great People, Both Women and Men Alike

Cindy has been fortunate to run across and meet some wonderful humans in her life, thanks to her work and diverse ongoing writing.

These humans have become leaders themselves by continuing to learn and grow in diverse ways.

In addition to special women that Cindy's been able to meet and keep in touch via, sharing their inspirational stories, Cindy's also known different men who have inspired her as well.

Chapter 1

Sister Jean Dolores Schmidt, Chaplain, Loyola Ramblers Basketball Team

Sister Jean Dolores Schmidt, Chaplain, Loyola Ramblers
(Photo Courtesy of Loyola University Chicago)

Cindy's shared some of her stories about going to school at Loyola University Chicago, where she did her master's degree in business administration.

She mentioned it was not easy because she had not taken any business classes while doing her first degree, a liberal arts bachelor's degree. But she graduated!

When we have talked about Loyola, I can tell Cindy really thought it was a great school, and then got involved in her alumni board.

But one incredibly special thing that has really made Cindy an avowed "Loyola gal" was when the Loyola Ramblers (basketball team) made it into the "Sweet Sixteen" in spring 2018. And then they made it into the Final Four. One inspiration part of this story was Sister Jean Dolores Schmidt, Chaplain for the Loyola Ramblers basketball team. Known as Sister Jean, she has served as Chaplain since 1994.

Sister Jean became a household name that year, and she was there at the games, providing inspiration, with her big smiles, charisma, pregame prayers, and pep talks. Cindy had a chance to interview Sister Jean via phone later in June 2018.

This was for a different book Cindy was writing focused on women executives. Cindy wanted to include Sister Jean's story, because she had mentored both young men and young women. And most of these women executives had actually been mentored in their careers by men.

More about Sister Jean's Background

When Cindy had a chance to do a personal phone call meeting with Sister Jean in June 2018, they spent time about Sister Jean's background.

Sister Jean explained more about of her background, growing up as a young girl. She told Cindy, "As a young girl, I felt I was called by God to be a nun, and I prayed about it. I also believed I wanted to be a teacher and a sister, so I entered the mother house in Dubuque, Iowa when I was 18."

Sister Jean then said, "I also had mentors. I honestly believe all of my teachers from grade school to high school were mentors, as were my mother and father along with my grandparents."

After joining the Blessed Virgin Mary in 1937, Sister Jean earned degrees at different schools in Los Angeles. Then she started teaching at several elementary schools for 20 years, along with serving as a principal. She also coached girls' sports. including basketball.

In 1961 Sister Jean then came to Chicago to work at Mundelein College where she held several different leadership positions. At that time, Mundelein College was an independent women's college, and was adjacent to Loyola University Chicago.

When Mundelein College merged with Loyola University Chicago in 1991, Sister Jean then became an academic advisor for Loyola's School of Continuing and Professional Studies.

How Becoming Chaplain of the Loyola Ramblers Came About

In 1994, Sister Jean retired from working full time but then she was asked to be the Loyola Ramblers' team Chaplain.

She mentioned, "Loyola invited me to accept this role because the priest who had served as Chaplain had retired from the university. So, I decided to accept it. Encouraging students has always been a part of my campus ministry at Loyola, helping them with their values, along with their future in life, as well as what they are called to do. This was another avenue for me to do this as Chaplain."

A Fun Fact about Sister Jean?

Sister Jean was actually a basketball player in her youth. Her role as Chaplain for the Loyola Ramblers let her combine her passion for mentoring and helping others with her love of basketball.

Her wonderful genuine smiles and cheering the Loyola Ramblers on through diverse ways not only inspired the basketball team. Sister Jean also managed to win the hearts of people watching the tournaments.

More about the Loyola Ramblers and Sister Jean Cheering Them On

In 2018, the Loyola Ramblers moved up into being one of the 16 basketball teams in the NCAA Finals. They were considered "underdogs" but then actually proceeded to be in the Final Four. During the games, Sister Jean continued to be there for the basketball team players.

Sister Jean's charisma, her genuine smile and pep talks with the team, cheering them on were part of how this highly active 98-year-old chaplain also won the hearts of people throughout the world as well.

When Sister Jean was not able to some of the games, she would send individual emails to each of the basketball players before and after the games. And when she attended the basketball games, she would lace up her custom-made Nikes® and huddle with the basketball team players, doing her pregame blessings and pep talks, along with cheering them on while she sat courtside.

When Cindy talked a bit more with Sister Jean, she shared more about these basketball team players. She said, "These are really good young men. They are unselfish and they truly like each other. They are not competitive with each other, but instead are competitive with the teams they play."

Although the Loyola Ramblers basketball team did not win the NCAA finals, with the coverage of the 2018 NCAA Tournament, Sister Jean became not only an inspiration to the Loyola Ramblers, but also because an inspiration to the world. She became a national focus with countless interviews.

Sister Jean's Words of Wisdom

While talking to Sister Jean, Cindy asked her, "Do you have any words of wisdom that would be good for people to keep in mind when they might be dealing with a challenge, whether it might be something physical or emotional?" Sister Jean said, "It goes back to the core of three important things – worship, work hard, and win."

Cindy continues to keep in touch with Sister Jean and in 2019 was able to attend the special Loyola University Chicago alumni's birthday celebration for Sister Jean, who turned 100 years old on August 21, 2019.

Loyola did this special event as an outdoor block party. During this special celebration, the people attending (including Cindy) also sang Happy Birthday to Sister Jean. Cindy told me it was an amazing celebration!

With the outbreak of Coronavirus, also known as COVID-19 in 2020, Loyola University Chicago instead did an online birthday celebration for Sister Jean, which Cindy was able to watch.

Cindy loves sending cards with special notes. Yes, she sent Sister Jean a special Birthday card for her August 21, 2020 birthday, and Sister Jean sent her a special thank you note via mail.

Cindy and I talked a bit more. Besides sending special cards, she also films short videos via a fantastic mobile app where the video gets embedded into the email. And Cindy has sent these sharing personal messages to Sister Jean, via emails.

Like Cindy, Sister Jean also uses different forms of communication, both via email and personalized notes that she mails out.

In the middle of December 2020, Cindy sent Sister Jean a Christmas card with a special note inside. On January 2, 2021, Sister Jean sent Cindy a special thank-you via email.

Cindy read me the special note that she got from Sister Jean. In it, she thanked Cindy for the lovely Christmas card and her message. Sister Jean then mentioned that it had been a difficult year, and why everyone wanted to welcome in 2021. She then said, "We are all looking forward to good health and to safety. Thank God for the vaccine. It should help a great deal."

Then Sister Jean continued on, saying, "Everyone is ready for peace and calm as well. We are not made for the constant turbulence we have had, nor have we been made for isolation. I believe that bringing students back to campus will be good for all concerned. I can hardly wait to return."

Sister Jean then ended her note and said, "May your 2021 be filled with many blessings and much happiness."

Sister Jean Dolores Schmidt with Cindy Bertram (Photo taken by Cindy Bertram)

Yes, Sister Jean has continued on her role as Chaplain for the Loyola Ramblers, and is truly an inspiration.

Chapter 2

How to Become Captain of a Ship – Celebrity Cruises® and Captain Kate McCue

Captain Kate McCue, Celebrity Cruises®
(Photo Courtesy of Celebrity Cruises®)

Cindy has actually met a few different cruise ship Captains while sailing on her cruises and they have all been wonderful. One of the most amazing Captains she has been fortunate to meet and talk with is Captain Kate McCue.

Captain Kate McCue is first American female captain of a mega-ton cruise ship. Cindy and I talked about this a bit more. I enjoy the water myself but have not sailed on a ship. Cindy not only enjoys taking cruises but loves sharing stories and writing about them.

Cindy actually had a chance to meet Captain Kate McCue when she was on the *Celebrity Edge*SM for a special naming ceremony. It took place on December 4,2018 and followed with a two-night post naming ceremony cruise.

Cindy loved enjoying and exploring the *Celebrity EdgeSM* for those extra days. She had a chance to see different areas of the ship, enjoy the phenomenal cuisine and diverse entertainment.

On the second day, Cindy mentioned she had a chance to enjoy lunch with another media friend, dining at a wonderful casual restaurant outside.
It was so relaxing, thanks to calm, blue ocean waters. Then Cindy went back inside, still enjoying the phenomenal views and started taking a few photos.

Captain Kate McCue happened to be onboard with another one of the Celebrity Cruises® bridge members for some special meetings. During a break they had from meetings, they were relaxing in some swinging chairs that were in the area Cindy had decided to explore. She said she thought she recognized Captain Kate as one of those two women.

So, Cindy walked over to them, and asked, "Are you by chance Captain Kate McCue? I've written about you." And Captain Kate began to smile and said, "Yes I am !" They chatted for a bit. Then Cindy was able to get a photo taken of her with Captain McCue.

After the photograph, Captain Kate and the other female bridge member went back relaxing a bit more in these swinging chairs. Cindy left smiling, because she was so thrilled and happy to have accidently met Captain Kate McCue. Cindy had actually written about Captain Kate McCue when she started at Celebrity Cruises® in 2015 as Captain of their *Celebrity Summit*®.

Cindy then shared more about Captain Kate McCue's background. Captain Kate became interested in sailing and cruise ships when her parents took the family on a vacation to the Bahamas. Kate was 12 years old at that time. She told her dad that she wanted to be a cruise director when she grew up. Her dad told her she could do anything she wanted to do and also encouraged her. And that is what started her dream career. Kate decided to attend the California Maritime Academy and graduated from there in 2002.

After graduating, however, it took longer for her to get a job. She got her application in to all the cruise lines but did not hear anything.

So, she decided to change her resume a bit, and applied to be a bartender. One cruise line told her she was not qualified to be a bartender. They saw her other qualifications, so she ended up joining that cruise line as a third mate.

After Kate worked for that cruise line as third mate for a bit, she then went to work for a different cruise line. And during the next 13 years, she worked her way up to becoming staff captain. Cindy explained that staff captain was actually a ship's second in command position.

Becoming the First Female Captain

Then in 2015, Captain Kate got a call from Celebrity Cruises®. They invited her to be their first female Captain, an offer she quickly accepted! And she served as Captain of their *Celebrity Summit* ®.

When Lisa Lutoff-Perlo became President and CEO of Celebrity Cruises® in December 2014, she wanted to make the recruitment and the promotion of women a focus. As a result, Celebrity Cruises® began recruiting in different ways – female cadets from the different maritime academies as well other avenues.

After serving as Captain of the *Celebrity Summit* ®, Captain Kate then became Captain of their *Celebrity Edge*SM.

In 2020, Celebrity Cruises® decided to do an industry first. On March 8, 2020, Celebrity Cruises® did a special cruise sailing on the *Celebrity Edge*sm. It featured an all-women bridge and officer team to celebrate International Women's Day. Captain Kate McCue was at the helm of that special cruise, and with her were women representing 16 different countries. And it was a phenomenal first that took place the cruise industry.

What Cindy and I loved about Captain Kate McCue's story? She never gave up and has continued on in her role as a Captain. She is a true inspiration.

Chapter 3

Genuine Leader & Cindy's "Pen Pal" - Richard Sasso, Chairman of MSC Cruises® USA

Richard Sasso, Chairman of MSC Cruises® USA
Photo Courtesy of MSC Cruises®

Cindy has met and kept in touch with some terrific executives due to her diverse writing and work tied to the cruise and travel industries. But one of her favorite stories is about Richard, "Rick" Sasso.

She first got to know Rick when he was Vice President of a cruise line that had more of an Italian ambiance. As Rick advanced in his career, he went over to a different cruise line company that started a new separate cruise line. And then he moved up becoming President and CEO of that cruise line.

In her work first as a travel advisor where she specialized in cruise sales, Cindy mentioned that yes, she got "hooked" on that new cruise line because they brought a new dimension to the cruise experience.

One area they focused on was cuisine, thanks to a partnership that cruise line established with a high-end, well-renowned Michelin chef. (Yes, Cindy enjoys cooking as well as more complicated cuisine!) And she fell in love with their ships because they continued to build new ones that were elegant and gorgeous !

As Cindy continued to attend different cruise conferences and events where Rick spoke and presented at special panels, she found he was very personable and extremely accessible.

She mentioned that she got to know Rick and if something came up where she wanted his insights, she would drop him a quick note, sometimes vial mail or email. And yes, he would get right back to her. Rick's fast turnround time getting back to her was amazing.

Rick's Caring and Genuine Leadership Style

One time Cindy had a group booked to sail on one the ships with the cruise line Rick was President and CEO of. As part of their Alaska package which included a three-night pre-cruise tour and then the Alaskan cruise, the cruise line booked the flights for the group members.

When she got the flight schedule for her group members, there were some challenging flight schedule times.

They were arriving extremely late that evening, and then the next morning had to be up and on an exceedingly early morning tour departure.

When Cindy reached out, the cruise line said they could not make any changes. She explained this to the group members, and they seemed to be okay with it.

Cindy thought it would be good to reach out to Rick and make him aware of this situation, so next year when their air/sea department was working the on flights to Alaska, the cruise line could maybe coordinate some better flight schedules for the cruise passengers. Cindy sent Rick a brief note about this but did not ask him for anything herself.

Just 8 days before her group was departing on their Alaskan cruise trip, Cindy got a call from the cruise line's air/sea department. They were able to get her group members booked on much better flights.

Later when she got the new airline tickets issued for her group members (and sent back the original airline tickets via express mail) she happened to ask the group department how this came about. And they said, "This came up through our President."

Cindy told me she that tears of joy came to eyes when she discovered how this had evolved. When she had reached out to Rick about this, she just wanted to let him know about this situation, so he could have his air/sea department staff work on this in the following year to improve flights. She was not expecting any last-minute flight changes for her group.

Cindy's Short Story Published in *Chicken Soup for the Traveler's Soul* Came About Through Rick's Help

Cindy and I have had some discussions on how sometimes things happen for a reason and a positive impact occurs. In my case, it was being adopted by my mom and dad, and during these past few years I love them even more each day.

Cindy shared a wonderful story that began when she was sailing on an Alaskan cruise.

She had gotten confirmed to do this Alaskan cruise last minute, and it was on the last sailing for that Alaskan cruising season. She told me that Alaskan cruises usually start in May and then end the first part of September before it gets too cold.

Cindy mentioned she got her dining set up just two days prior to the ship's departure and was able to get a large table. She likes to talk to different people during dinner. Also, Cindy got her late dining time confirmed. Unlike me, who likes to have dinner at 6 pm each night, Cindy likes to eat a bit later.

When Cindy went to the dining room for dinner the first night of the cruise, people started coming in and sat down. Then a young man in a non-motorized wheel chair came and sat in the space next to Cindy. It appeared he did not have a left arm.

They started talking. His name was Mike, and it turned out he was going to be going back to the University of California after the cruise and take the last classes needed to get his degree in business.

They had a fun discussion about this because Cindy had gotten her Master's in Business Administration from Loyola University Chicago.

Mike left the dining room after eating his dinner and his parents stayed. They explained that nine months before, Mike had been involved in a near fatal car crash where he was an innocent victim. The woman who hit him had fallen asleep at the wheel of her car, and Mike ended up surviving but lost his left arm at the shoulder and his left leg above the knee.
His family had set up a trust fund to help pay for his prosthetic limbs.

Mike's energy and positivity throughout the cruise really impressed Cindy. He got off at all the ports of call and was using a wheelchair. Cindy wanted to find a way to help with the trust fund efforts.
Just a few months prior to taking this cruise she had gotten a letter from Rick, thanking her for some positive feedback she had sent him in a detailed letter. And he told her in that letter if she ever needed anything, to feel free to contact him.

Well, the cruise line she was sailing on was the one that Rick was President of, so when she got back from the cruise? She sent Rick a personal letter mentioning that she had met Mike and shared a bit more about his story. Cindy asked if maybe the cruise line Rick was President of might donate a cruise to Mike's Trust Fund, and this would be raffled off. Then the proceeds/funds would then being put into this account to help pay for his prosthetic limbs. She also included a few photos of Mike that she had taken of him on that cruise.

Just three weeks after sending Rick the letter and photos? She got a call from that cruise line and they donated a cruise to be raffled off, raising money for Mike's Trust Fund.
This cruise that was donated and raffled off raised over $25,000 and this money was then put into that special Trust Fund set up for Mike.

 Cindy also shared this story in a few articles she wrote, and also kept Rick updated on how Mike was doing. Mike had gone back to college and was taking classes to finish his degree.

Rick wound up coming into Chicago for a special dinner event (this was for travel professionals) and they chatted more. And Rick offered to work on getting another cruise donated to Mike's Trust Fund that could be raffled off. Cindy got confirmation of this second cruise being donated to Mike's Trust Fund just 3 days before she flew out to attend Mike's graduation!

She mentioned she was so excited to attend Mike's graduation. He had gotten fitted with his new prosthetic left leg and actually walked at graduation! Later Cindy noticed that a new book was being pulled together and decided to submit a short story. She got the short story written, sent it in, after making it through the process? Her short story was one of the 101 stories included in this book. Her short story, "A Cruise and a Promise" was in *Chicken Soup for the Traveler's Soul.*

Cindy mentioned this story would not have occurred had it not been for Rick's help and that cruise line's generosity.

Moving on in his Career – Leading Another Cruise Line

As far as Rick's career? Cindy mentioned that at the end of 2001, Rick left that one cruise line he had been President and CEO of for several years. He continued to keep his hands in the business world via diverse ways.

Then in 2004 Rick became President, MSC Cruises® USA.

Positioning MSC Cruises® USA for greater growth and recognition in the North American market was a key area MSC Cruises® USA wanted to achieve and where Rick's expertise and leadership was needed

Over the past years, MSC Cruises® USA has been working extremely hard to build their presence in the North American cruise market.

And they have also focused on growing the number of travel professional advisors who work with them.

Rick shared some key things with Cindy. He said, "It's about the human factor. There is a people connection, and we are continuing to take that to the next level."

Cindy mentioned that she and Rick had a great discussion one time about luck.

As far as being lucky, Rick explained, "You hear people say, 'I was lucky.' What they should have understood is that it is only luck if you don't deserve the reward." Then Rick then said, "But if you make decisions that eventually gave you a lucky opportunity, then you made that luck. So, you have to make luck. And this comes in many forms of action."

In August of 2016, Rick assumed the role as Chairman of MSC Cruises® USA. MSC Cruises® USA continues to grow, building new ships and offering diverse itineraries throughout the world. They have also continued growing the awareness of people in the North American cruise market.

Rick has been nationally recognized with awards. In 1999, Rick was named "Cruise Industry Executive of the Year," by a leading travel industry trade magazine. And in 2011, Rick received the "Hall of Fame" recognition from the Cruise Lines International Association (also known as CLIA).

Rick has spent almost his entire career life in the cruise industry, and his passion for it definitely shows.

As Far as Being Pen Pals?

As far as being pen pals? I looked up the term "pen pals" to see what it meant. It first began describing people who regularly would write to each other.

As far as how Cindy and Rick got to be pen pals? Cindy would correspond with Rick, and he always got back to her quickly. Over the years, their communicating regularly transformed from written letters to emails and text messages, along with other forms of communication.

Cindy shared a fun story with me. While at a special cruise conference, Cindy happened to see Rick coming out of a meeting with another cruise line executive. She went over to say hi, and Rick introduced Cindy to this executive. Then this executive turned to Rick and asked him, "Well, who is Cindy?" Rick told him, "Oh, she's my pen pal."

Cindy and Rick continue keeping in touch via diverse ways – phone calls, emails, and text messages. He appreciates the ongoing diverse articles Cindy's written and had published over the years.

Giving Back and Having a Positive Impact – His Book, *UNSELFISHWORLD*

Rick has a passion for giving back and having a positive impact in many diverse ways. One? He wrote a book himself, *UNSELFISHWORLD.* In it, he encouraged people to be unselfish and have a positive impact. His book included wonderful stories, and Cindy shared a few of those with me.

One of the stories Cindy read to me was about a long flight Rick took where he quietly did a wonderful act of kindness. Yes, this true story captured my heart.

The story? Rick was taking a long flight. Once he got to his assigned seat on the plane, he thought about maybe reading a book and relaxing. Then several soldiers came down the aisle and filled the vacant seats.

One of these soldiers sat near Rick. Rick asked him where they were heading off to. This soldier mentioned they were going for two weeks of special training in Petawawa, and then they would be going to Afghanistan.

After flying for about an hour, an announcement was made that sack lunches were available for a fee. (They were not free lunches.) Rick thought getting a sack lunch would be good, because there were several hours left on this flight.

Rick overhead one of the soldiers quietly mention
to another soldier that the price seemed a bit
expensive and said he would just pass and wait til
they got to their base. Rick also noticed that none of
the other soldiers ordered sack lunches.

Rick quietly walked to the back of the plane, handed
cash to the flight attendant, and asked her to take
sack lunches to all the soldiers onboard. Tears came
to her eyes, and she got those prepaid lunches to
those 10 soldiers on the flight.

Later on this flight, Rick mentioned he was heading to
the restroom and another gentleman stopped Rick.
He quietly said he had seen what Rick had done for
those soldiers. He wanted to help, and quietly gave
Rick some cash.

And then when Rick walked towards the front of the
plane to stretch his legs, another man wanted to
shake Rick's hand and quietly gave him some cash.

The plane landed and Rick gathered his belongings to disembark. While waiting by the airplane door, another man stopped Rick, and quietly put something in his shirt pocket. It was more cash.

When Rick entered the terminal, he saw those soldiers gathering together, waiting for the transportation to take them to their base. Rick went over to those soldiers and handed them the cash all those other people had quietly given him. Rick told these soldiers that he knew it was probably going to take them some time to get to the base and they would probably need another sandwich. Then Rick said, "God Bless You."

This story brought tears to Cindy's eyes as well as mine.

And although I have not met Rick myself yet? He truly is an extraordinary, wonderful, caring human being. His book, *UNSELFISHWORLD* is just one example.

Rick's ongoing acts of kindness, genuinely caring about others, working extremely hard, leading by example and his genuine leadership are more reasons why he shines, and continues to have a positive impact in the world.

Chapter 4

Learning the Human Touch – Herbert Kelleher, Co-Founder of Southwest Airlines Co.

Herbert Kelleher, Co-Founder, Southwest Airlines Co.
(Photo courtesy of Southwest Airlines Co.)

Herbert Kelleher, the Co-Founder of Southwest Airlines Co., is someone that Cindy greatly admired, and she shared more about him, along with how he created the most successful airline in history.

Herbert was also affectionately known as Herb. He was not only the co-founder of Southwest Airlines Co., but served as President and CEO, and later Chairman. Herb was actually a highly successful attorney and had his legal practice in San Antonio. One evening in1966, Herb met with one of his clients, Rollin King, who had an idea for a new business.

That evening Herb and Rollin sketched out a rough idea for Southwest Airlines on a cocktail napkin. Their pulse? They wanted to make this a successful low fare airline in Texas. (Rollin, by the way, became a co-founder of Southwest Airlines with Herb.)

Herb put in some of his own money to get Southwest Airlines started.

After getting authorized to fly by the Texas Aeronautics Commission, other airline carriers wanted to shut down Southwest Airlines and went to court. But Herb and Rollin did not stop. Herb continued the battle with the Texas Supreme Court, and he won.

Southwest Airlines got off the ground and started in 1971. But the other airline carriers started to battle Southwest Airlines in a new way. They started a pricing war, where they cut their airfare prices.

Southwest Airlines made it through this, and in 1973 they posted a profit. Then in 1978, Herb was named President of the Board, and in 1982 he became CEO as well.

How Cindy Got Connected with Herb Kelleher?

Cindy told me that she has always been a big fan of Southwest Airlines herself. She said that Herb Kelleher was featured as the front cover story of a major business magazine's May 28, 2001 issue. Herb was getting ready to step down as the CEO and President of Southwest Airlines in June but was going to remain on as Chairman.

Cindy sent Herb a personal letter and in it besides including some key things she loved about Southwest Airlines? Cindy shared a story about one of the Southwest Airlines employees who went above and beyond helping one of her clients. At that time, besides her ongoing diverse writing, Cindy also worked as a travel advisor for full-service retail travel agency. Herb Kelleher sent a beautiful letter to Cindy.

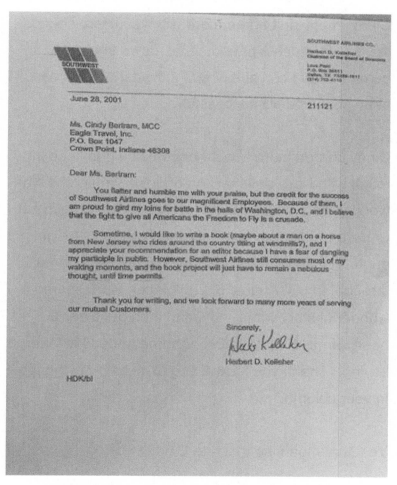

Herbert Kelleher's letter to Cindy Bertram

In Herb Kelleher's June 28, 2001, letter to Cindy, he truly reinforced all the positive thoughts she had. Cindy read Herb Kelleher's letter to me, and I could see that he truly was a caring, down to earth, tremendous leader who led by example. And I told Cindy, "I couldn't agree more with you. Herb sounds like he was such a phenomenal, down to earth human. Now I can see why Southwest Airlines has been so incredibly successful."

Cindy shared more about her continuing to keep in touch with Herb Kelleher. An ongoing writer, she was working on a future column and decided to reach out to Herb Kelleher to see if she might be able to get a quote from him to include. Once again Herb came through. In his August 5, 2001 letter, Herb shared a wonderful story with Cindy, and then gave her a heartwarming quote to use. And he ended his letter saying, "Thank you for wanting to include my thoughts in your column."

Yes, that meant so much to Cindy !

Herb's Impressive Work and Leadership Style

Herb's letters to Cindy displayed his work and leadership style. Responding back to Cindy in such a quick time, and then later giving her a quote to use showed his leadership style.

He was very accessible, and it was apparent that he genuinely cared about people. And at Southwest Airlines, he created "a culture of commitment."

A few examples of Herb's style? Cindy mentions she ran across several examples and shared these with me. Herb was known for inviting employees to a weekly Friday cookout. And he also would work with the Southwest Airlines' employees handling baggage during the Thanksgiving holidays rush.

And Herb would show up at company gatherings, sometimes riding in on a motorcycle, dressed up as a well-known celebrity singer, singing one of artist's award-winning songs.

Creating and Building wonderful Culture

Herb created and built a wonderful culture at Southwest Airlines. He believed that it was possible run an airline providing fantastic service, be successful and make money, but also love people, both customers and employees alike and have fun.

Putting Employees First

When creating Southwest Airlines, a key area Herb focused on was making sure employees came first. He felt that happy employees would lead to happy clients, and this was something his mother had taught him.

Herb's passion, his zest for life, having a wonderful sense of humor and being such a caring person were all parts of what he built at Southwest Airlines. He wanted to create a culture that inspired passionate people coming to work fully engaged in what they did and loving what they did.

Successfully Getting Through Unexpected Challenges

Something else that impressed Cindy about Herb Kelleher and Southwest Airlines? After the tragedies of 9/11 occurred (September 11, 2001), it was an extremely challenging time for the airlines. Other major airlines were trying to get bailout money from the US Federal government, but Southwest Airlines did not take that approach.

Cindy told me Southwest Airlines did not ask for any bailout money. They got through this challenging situation themselves and also made sure that none of their employees lost their jobs.

Southwest Airlines' Culture and Positivity

In Herb's 30+ years, first starting Southwest Airlines and then building it beyond a low-cost airline and the continued growth?

Herb's focusing on their employees became a core part of what also made Southwest Airlines so extremely successful.

Herb also won countless awards, including repeatedly being voted as the best CEO in the airline industry. He really changed the world in an incredibly positive way.

Herb's passion, his zest for life, contagious sense of humor, and being an entertaining storyteller were key things he was well known for.

Herb died on January 3, 2019,at the age of 87. He was loved by so many people, and his legend continues to live on.

Herb Kelleher's inspiration, his leadership style, focusing on their employees and beliefs that happy employees would lead to happy clients are why Southwest Airlines has been a true success.

And this continues on today. During their fifty years of existence and operations, they have never had to downsize or layoff any of their employees. On June 18, 2021, Southwest Airlines Co. also did a special 50th anniversary celebration being in business.

And what Herbert Kelleher created lives on.

Chapter 5

How to Be a Great Business Tiger...John P. Imlay, Jr.

Cindy had run across a book that captured her attention because she loved the name! The book was *Jungle Rules: How to Be a Tiger in Business™* written by John Imlay, Jr. with Dennis Hamilton.

Cindy and I started talking about tigers and how they were a bit of a different breed as far as animals. (I am a dog myself.) A tiger is a much bigger than a cat. Male tigers can weight from 200 to 680 pounds, and female tigers can weight anywhere from 140 to 370 pounds.

Cindy and I then found out a few more facts about tigers. They are nocturnal, which means they are more active at night. And thanks to their dark vertical stripes on the orangish brown fur, their stripes provide a camouflage. Their striped coats help them blend in well within their surroundings, and they are also difficult to be seen from unsuspecting prey.

Tigers have sharp eyesight along with very acute senses. And a tiger is known as being a symbol of power.

Cindy then shared some sections about what was in the book and how it related to success in business. I could see why it grabbed her attention because it was fascinating!

More About John Imlay, Jr.

John Imlay, Jr. had years of business experience and was a technology pioneer, a philanthropist, extremely successful businessman, an entrepreneur, and a family man with many passions.

After working for several companies, John took command of an independent software company, Management Science America, also known as MSA. Based in Atlanta, Georgia, MSA was on the brink of bankruptcy. But just ten years later, John Imlay, Jr. was able to build MSA into a phenomenally successful company. It became the largest independent software company in the world.

Under John's leadership, the company grew from generating $2 million in revenue to $280 million in revenue by 1989. Then Dun & Bradstreet Corporation indicated they wanted to buy the company. MSA was sold to Dun & Bradstreet Corporation for $333 million and John directed the merger. He then served as chairman until 1996 when he retired.

His passion for other areas, including philanthropy continued. John formed Imlay Investments as well as the Imlay Foundation. The Imlay Foundation became a mainstay of philanthropy. At Imlay Investments John worked with more than 100 technology companies as an angel investor.

John Imlay, Jr.'s Book – *Jungle Rules: How to Be a Tiger in Business*™

John Imlay, Jr. then decided to share more of what he had learned during his years working in corporate management and why he wrote his book, using a unique approach.

John felt people were the key when it came to success in business – the competitive jungle.

In the introduction of his book, John mentioned that after finishing college he first set his foot in what he called the "business jungle."

As far as the term "jungle" this meant the environment that businesses operated in. John started to create "Jungle Rules" because these applied to a certain type ("breed") of people who were unconquerable, persisted on, and never stopped until they were able to achieve their goals.

John called them "tigers" – they were able to figure out how to win at their businesses. A key part of their success involved the relationships they had with people.

John then shared 20 different Jungle Rules in the chapters of his book. One of Cindy's favorites was in Chapter 11, titled Relationships for Fun and Profit. And it included John's *"Jungle Rule #11 - Build a front porch on your treehouse."*

Cindy read that chapter to me, and it really made a great deal of sense. I do enjoy sitting on a front porch, watching humans walk by, sometimes with their kids who had 2 feet, as well as ones like me with 4 feet. A front porch was a good way to really engage with people, speak with the neighbors, and develop ongoing relationships.

But later people started to transition into building decks in their back yards, along with putting up fences.

And this seemed to also transition into the business world as well. Companies seemed to isolate themselves, putting up new "fences," along with being extremely impersonal.

As far as John Imlay, Jr.? He believed and stressed the need for "incessant personal interaction," and this was a part of how he was able to build Management Science America (MSA) into an extremely successfully company.

He believed in the need to have interactive relationships, via in-person conversations as well as phone calls.

At Management Science America, John Imlay, Jr. created that front porch and through this, still managed to successfully keep this big business stay small enough with that human interaction !

He also believed in making things personal and growing true relationships. John Imlay, Jr. also felt that if someone contacted you personally, then they should receive a personal response back.

Some key things John mentioned that needed to be part of building that front porch on your treehouse? He said that it was important to make sure your business was set up to interact with people. He also felt that making life friendly and then having loyalty be a backbone of the relationship were also extremely important. Also, it was critical to make your interactions personal and doing the right thing, even if it was not something in the company's handbook.

Doing the Right Thing

Another point John focused on was making sure you did the right thing. And he shared a story in his book.

John mentioned that an employee of his came to him because he was facing a very rough and tragic dilemma. This man's wife, who was only thirty-two years old, had been diagnosed with an extremely severe form of breast cancer. She had been told that the only treatment available which might save her life was a specialized bone marrow transplant. Without this, she only had a few months left to live. But the cost of this specialized treatment was $150,000.

This employee then mentioned he had talked with the insurance company about this – his wife's diagnosis, and the recommendations from her physician for this specialized bone marrow transplant.

But the agents at the insurance company told him they could not cover the cost of this treatment because it was considered "experimental."

John called the president of this insurance company, but the insurance company would not budge.

John called his employee in. He told him to call the doctor and have that surgery for his wife scheduled and done as soon as possible. John then said that they (the company) would pay the medical bill and then fight with the insurance company. The surgical procedure was able to put that woman's cancer in remission. And in the meantime, John and the company were able to settle things with that insurance company, and they covered half of the bill.

What John did in just that one example about doing the right thing really captured our hearts.

It made complete sense to Cindy and me, and I really loved that Jungle Rule about building a front porch on your treehouse.

Cindy also read the last chapter of John Imlay, Jr.'s book to me.

This was his Conclusion. He mentioned that although he covered and included twenty rules in his book? There really was one key message – that it was about the people. People were really the key to the success.

Cindy loved John's book and learned so many terrific things after reading it. Cindy used some key points that John Imlay, Jr. had focused on and included these in a diverse article she wrote and then had published. And Cindy showed me that special article and it really resonated me as well.

Then Cindy sent John a copy of the article along with a note. John sent her back a special autographed hard bound copy of his book. In. In the autograph message he said, "To Cindy, The positive impact Tiger!"

Cindy loved this and showed me the autographed copy of his book he had sent her.

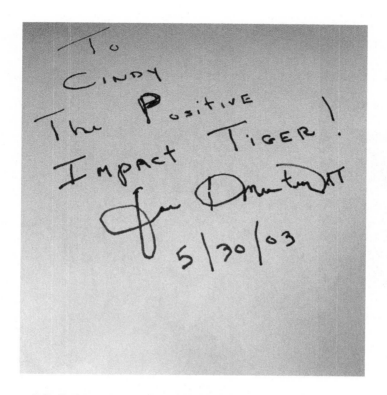

John Imlay Jr.'s special autograph to Cindy Bertram

This made Cindy smile so much. And having known her for a while, along with knowing some of the accomplishments she has done? She truly is that positive impact Tiger !

Chapter 6

Successfully Walking on a new Foot – Cindy's mom, Ruth

Photo of Ruth, Cindy's mom
(Photo of Ruth taken by Cindy Bertram)

While sharing more about our families, Cindy and I both talked about how we grew up as kids.

I was a puppy who became a dog, and Cindy was a young girl who then became a young lady and adult human.

An area where we really connected was talking about our moms. In my case, it was going from having a physical mom (she was a grown-up dog) to a human mom, Jodee. In Cindy's case, Cindy's been lucky to have a great human mom, Ruth.

Cindy's mom, Ruth, always worked hard, and had a few different careers. After first working as a cashier in a supermarket, she got into doing bookkeeping. From there, she moved into different areas and later owned a full-service retail travel agency. After owning that business and running it for several years, Ruth decided to retire.

Unexpected – Dealing with Heel Cancer

Then something unexpected came up. A year after retiring, a spot came up on the heel of Ruth's right foot, and it turned out to be a cancerous spot.

Cindy mentioned that after it was diagnosed, her mom and dad went to Mayo Clinic. The doctors told Ruth that Friday morning they could not just remove the cancerous tissue spot. The doctors said they were going to have to amputate her right foot below the knee.

They got the surgery scheduled on that upcoming Monday morning. Cindy said her mom was worried about the surgery, because if the cancer had already spread, she did not want to lose her right leg.

Fortunately, the cancer had not spread, and the surgery was a success. When Cindy's mom came out of the surgery, she was still feeling the effects of the anesthesia. But the first thing she told her husband, Cindy's dad? Ruth said, "When I get fitted with my fake foot, I'm going to Disney World™, and I'm taking my daughters !"

Going through the post-surgery recuperation was not easy because it was a bit painful, but Cindy mentioned that her mom made it through this. And she and her family were also quietly worried on how Ruth would handle this emotionally.

Her Next Steps

Ruth had always been extremely active her whole life. She got fitted with the prosthetic leg, and a few months later was walking around like a pro.

Something else she did was get the hand controls put on her car. Then she went through some training how to use these (since she did not have a real right foot to drive with) and was able to drive her car again.

Planning a Special Trip

And sticking to those first words she muttered to Cindy's dad after she was coming out of the anesthesia after surgery? Ruth actually took Cindy, Cindy's sisters, her two granddaughters and her grandson to Walt Disney World™ a few months later for an incredibly special trip.

This was Ruth's first vacation since becoming an amputee. But everything just fell into place. It was later in the summer. They flew down to Orlando and got checked into their hotel at Walt Disney World™ where they would be staying for the next 5 days. Cindy's mom did have a cane with her, and they also brought Ruth's wheelchair along for her to use as needed.

They had a fun time watching the parades, along with going on the different rides.

Cindy mentioned her mom would hop out of the wheelchair, and use her cane walking over to get on the different rides. And she was able to meet some of the Disney™ characters.

Photo of Mickey Mouse™ with Ruth
(Photo taken by Cindy Bertram)

A Funny "Role Reversal" During this Trip

Then a funny "role reversal" occurred during that week while they were enjoying this special Disney World™ vacation.

Cindy's youngest niece, Evie, was 11 years old at the time. She "overdid it" a bit with dinner the third evening of their trip. The next morning, Evie complained about not feeling well. She said she was too sick to go to visit the park and wanted to stay in the hotel room. So, Cindy, her mom, her other sister Jodee, along with Evie's sister, and Cindy's nephew went to the park that morning to enjoy another fun day together.

Later, after resting up, Evie finally told her mom she would go to the park but only if her mom rented her a wheel chair to use, so she would not get tired with all the walking.

They met Cindy's mom and family at the park. Evie seemed a bit somber, so Ruth decided to get her in a better mood. Ruth grabbed the wheelchair that Evie was sitting in and started pushing her fast to the next ride they were all going on. Cindy then said, "Yes, we were left with our mom's wheelchair, which was empty, and we pushed it, trying to play catch-up to make that next ride!"

Cindy mentioned, "We had an amazing time during this special trip to Walt Disney World™. And watching my mom being so active on that trip, navigating all these parks literally walking on a new leg was amazing !"

It was proof that nothing was going to hold Ruth back! Ruth's being able to do Walt Disney World™ with a new foot was incredible.

Chapter 7

You Made Day! ...Gary Sain, Former President & CEO, Visit Orlando

In an era today, where machines are being built replacing positions held by humans? It is even more important that humans do not turn into machines and robots themselves.

Cindy and I were discussing this, and one of the stories she shared occurs when she has to call her cell phone provider. They have machines (instead of humans) in place, that attempt to answer questions, but most of the time it does not work well.

She has told me, "When this occurs, I would rather just speak with a real human and not a machine, because they can help me much better."

Cindy is one who does not want to act like a machine herself. Being personal, yet professional along with building relationships is extremely important to her.

She then shared more about one human who really demonstrated this so well himself, Gary Sain.

Cindy first got to know Gary when he was Senior Vice President, Sales, Marketing & Passenger Services for a cruise line, Premier Cruise Lines, which was also known as The Big Red Boat.

Gary Sain had a diverse, extraordinarily successful background in the hospitality and travel industry. He had worked for some well-known hotel corporations in sales and marketing vice president positions. And he brought this to his role at Premier Cruise Lines.

Cindy had an opportunity to meet Gary when he came to Chicago for a special presentation event. Then she sent him a letter as a follow-up. Gary actually mailed Cindy a personal note and in it, he said, "You made my day."

What impressed Cindy was the fact that he took the time to send her a note. It really showcased the fact that he was a real human, truly genuine and took the extra time building relationships on all levels.

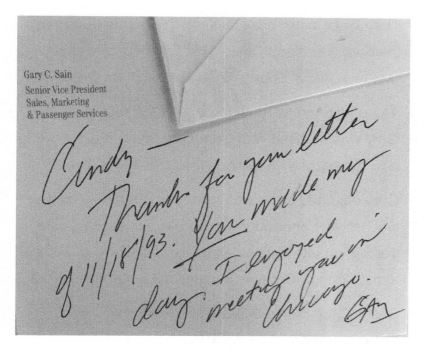

Gary Sain's special note to Cindy Bertram

Gary eventually left his role working at that cruise line, and then became executive vice-president, chief marketing officer and partner of a well-known Orlando-based international advertising and public relations agency.

Cindy and Gary kept in touch periodically, via notes, emails, and phone calls. She mentioned he was always encouraging her as far as her career, and professional growth.

Then Gary joined Visit Orlando in February 2007 as their president and CEO. Visit Orlando, by the way, was the Official Tourism Association® for Orlando.

His energy continued, and one of his successes? Gary was credited with Orlando actually reaching a new record of 51.5 million visitors in 2010.

Gary also had other wonderful achievements as well. One he was enormously proud of was successfully getting an international industry tradeshow to be held at the Orange County Convention Center April 2012.

Sadly, Gary Sain died very suddenly and unexpectedly on May 4, 2012.

But Cindy still has the note he had sent her back in 1993 and mentions it is a positive that shares a great human's mindset – "You made my day."

Chapter 8

Opening a Door and Changing a Life... Patricia Rickard, Epic Enterprise Tours

Photo of Patricia Rickard, Epic Enterprise Tours
(Photo of Patricia Rickard taken by Cindy Bertram)

When it comes to meeting great humans, sometimes it really happens when you cross paths with someone and meet that human for a reason. Cindy and I talked quite a bit about this.

She shared more about another great human, Patricia "Pat" Rickard, who wound up becoming a very dear friend of hers. She and Pat had met at a cruise conference in 2003 and they just seemed to "click."

Patricia's Expertise

Patricia's 50 years of expertise working in the travel industry as a travel advisor and then later owning her own professional travel agency business was fascinating. When Patricia, "Pat", was 20 years old, she put together and personally escorted a group of 81 guests on a transatlantic cruise from the United States to Great Britain. In 1953, Pat organized another group of 50 guests who did a transatlantic cruise over to Great Britain. They wanted to visit relatives. Then they did another transatlantic cruise sailing back to the US.

Pat then went to college, and after graduating, she started teaching at Fullerton College.

The classes she taught included business management, world tourism and service transportation.

While teaching there, however, Pat found that some of the textbooks did not really cover everything needed. And this was one of the driving forces behind her setting up her own travel agency, Epic Enterprise Tours Inc. in 1980. Not only did she use this as a learning tool for her students, but she also expanded her agency's presence and sales in different areas.

Pat first started creating day trips. Then she expanded the business by growing her expertise in new areas. She also got key credentials.

Getting her CTC™ Certified Travel Counselor was just one. She also went through and completed courses to get certifications through the Cruise Lines International Association, also known as CLIA.

Taking on More Roles and Being Active in the Community

Pat also grew her involvement in the community along with taking on more professional roles. She became a member of SKAL International USA, a Professional Organization of Global Tourism Leaders.

She was also founder of the Orange County Women in Travel and served as membership Vice President of IFWTO, the International Federation of Women's Travel Organization. As a result of these different roles, Pat was a recipient of the Key to the City of Manila.

Owning Epic Enterprise Tours, Inc., Pat traveled extensively throughout the world. Another part of her traveling came about when she married her husband Ernie, who was an airline pilot and served in the U.S. Air Force.

One Special Story

Pat was also very adamant about giving back – acts of kindness, donating her time, and creating fundraising events.

A story that Cindy shared with me about Pat was so heartwarming. Pat was doing some volunteer work at a hospital at the time, and this was during the Vietnam War.

In her volunteer role there, Pat had a book cart that she pushed around.

This cart had free books that the hospital patients could take and read. Then she would pick up those books when the patients finished reading them. As I mentioned to Cindy, this seemed like a movable library !

As Pat was sharing books with the hospital patients, she walked by a patient's room and the door was closed. After talking with the nurses in that section of the hospital, they explained that the hospital patient in that room was a young soldier who had been injured in the Vietnam War. He was recuperating but was very depressed. And this is why he kept the door closed. Pat then asked the nurses if she could help and then explained what she wanted to do. And they told her, "Go for it!"

So, what did Pat do? She would push the book cart by that young man's room and then would stop. Then she would open the door slightly but would quickly shut the door !

Pat continued to do this, and each time she would open the door a bit more. Finally, after a few weeks, she finally opened the door completely. She walked in and said, "Let's talk." This young man opened up to Pat, and through this discussion as well as more of their talks that continued? Pat was able to get this young man to come out of his depression. And he actually started helping other injured soldiers (including veterans) come out of their own state of depression.

This truly was a random act of kindness that had a positive impact on a young soldier's life.

And as Cindy and both agreed? By opening that door, Pat did help change a young soldier's life for the better.

This was just one of many ways Patricia gave back to others, and Cindy mentioned she was so grateful that she and Patricia met randomly, became dear friends, and worked to help others.

Chapter 9

The Architect of the River Cruise Industry...Rudi Schreiner, President and Co-Founder of AmaWaterways™

Rudi Schreiner, President & Co-Founder, AmaWaterways™

(Photo Courtesy of AmaWaterways™)

When Cindy and I chat about traveling, she gets extremely energetic and excited when the topic of cruising comes up. As far as the cruise industry, one area that has evolved and continued to grow has been the river cruise industry.

Cindy explained a bit more to me about what differentiates the river cruise industry. And then she mentioned one phenomenal person, Rudi Schreiner, who truly is "The architect of the cruise industry."

In our discussion, Cindy shared more about Rudi Schreiner, President and Co-Founder of AmaWaterways™. Rudi really helped turn river cruising from a niche into one of the fastest growing segments in this industry.

Born in Vienna, the capital of Austria, which is located on the Danube River, Rudi's love for design drew him into architecture, which he studied at a university.

Rudi also loved traveling. So, he got his Passport, and then spent 7 months on the road, where he wrote articles for newspapers.

Rudi then came to the United States. He planned and did several trips. Then he traveled to South America for a special journalism assignment on the Amazon While there, Rudi actually built a raft that took him up and down the river.

He also spent time doing research that was focused on how changes in society changed architecture.

Then Rudi moved to the United States where he lived in New Orleans and worked there along with doing his Master of Business Administration (MBA) degree.

In 1982, Rudi opened up his own tour company, Student Travel International, located in California. A few of his friends were in the tour business, and they got together to form this company. Student Travel International planned student tours from the United States to Europe.

Then in 1990 he started his next company, Amadeus International Tours which was based in Calabasas, California.

When the Gulf War started, it disrupted existing tours, and Rudi was then hired by a company to develop a new product for them. It was tied into connecting the Rhine with the Danube and was originally for industrial purposes as far as freight and barge shipping. But then it allowed opportunities for long distance cruising as well.

In 1993, Rudi put together the first programs for this company and it involved river cruising. It continued to grow, and by 2000, this company had close to 20,000 river cruise guests.

Rudi left that company in 2000 and started Viking River Cruises with a group of 15 people. They chartered ships.

How the Creation of AmaWaterways™ Came About

In 2002, Rudi started having discussions with Jimmy Murphy, an extremely brilliant and successful travel entrepreneur. Jimmy Murphy had built Brendan Vacations into being one of the most successful tour operators in the U.S. In their discussions, Jimmy Murphy mentioned they could create a new river cruise line company themselves. As Rudi and Jimmy continued working on creating this new river cruise line, Kristin Karst came in. As one of the three founders, Kristin's extensive and diverse experience in travel, handling customer service and river cruising provided more.

Rudi shared more and explained, "When Kristin, Jimmy Murphy and I sat down to dream up the perfect river cruise company, we shared a vision of inviting guests to discover the spectacular scenery and enchanting towns along the world's most iconic rivers in a style that was luxurious yet warm and friendly."

They decided to start AmaWaterways™ in 2002 and began by leasing one ship from another river cruise line operator.

Rudi mentioned that even at the very beginning, he, Kristin, and Jimmy focused on their goal of creating a river cruise company that they themselves would also enjoy.

After starting AmaWaterways™ they began building their own unique one-of-a-kind ships.

AmaWaterways™ focused on incorporating the comforts and conveniences. Having the highest-quality sourced food and wine on their elegantly appointed ships, staterooms that offered maximum views was one part.

Also, their signature view-enhancing twin balconies and their unique, one and only Chef's Table specialty restaurant became key things that AmaWaterways™ focused on. Another? Having crew members who went above and beyond.

AmaWaterways™ has continued successfully growing and launching new river cruise line ships since then. And they are still family owned. Jimmy Murphy's son, Gary, who had played a major part in Brendan Vacations' success, also came in as Senior Vice President of Sales, a role he continues to hold today.

In 2014, Jimmy Murphy passed away. But the innovative features, and firsts that evolved in 2002 when Rudi, Kristin and Jimmy worked on creating AmaWaterways™ has continued on.

Continuing on with New Firsts

Cindy mentioned that when speaking with Rudi, they went over some new "firsts" in the river cruise industry that AmaWaterways™ began introducing. One was the introduction of providing complimentary bicycles for guests to use.

Then Rudi shared more about the continuation AmaWaterways™ has done, elevating the experiences for their guests.

Rudi explained, "We were the first river cruise line to carry a fleet of 25 bicycles onboard our ships. We wanted to provide guests with an alternative to the walking shore excursions and felt that many would enjoy bicycling through the city or countryside. Today we are seeing an enormous amount of growth in the active travel area – not just biking but also hiking tours."

Rudi then said, "Many guests want to continue their healthy active lifestyle while onboard, and it's our pleasure to provide them with a range of options to do that. In addition, we offer guests healthy food options onboard with our 'healthy corner,' gem-waters and gluten-free, low-sodium and vegan options. "

Designing and More Firsts

Rudi looked at all the designs and wanted to include key things onboard for their guests to enjoy. These included providing free Wi-Fi for all their guests onboard, more dining options, and a focus on health and wellness, in addition to more space for guests to enjoy.

Other firsts that are part of AmaWaterways™? Their innovative stateroom design, which features "twin balconies" is one, as well as their diverse shore excursions which feature hiking and biking options for the active traveler. Another? Many of their ships have heated outdoor swimming pools onboard that feature swim-up bars.

Utilizing his Architect Expertise

Using his diverse architectural expertise and skills, besides his having successfully built other companies, are additional strengths Rudi has brought to AmaWaterways™.

Rudi has designed and then created their new "one of a kind" river cruise line ships with revolutionary details. And this is what has also helped accelerate AmaWaterways™ to a completely new level.

A wonderful example of Rudi's architectural expertise and bringing innovation to river cruising? It was his design of their *AmaMagna,* which is actually twice the width of other more traditional river ships.

More on AmaWaterways™ and Their Continued Success

Founded in 2002, the AmaWaterways™ fleet has continued to grow to over 25 custom-designed ships sailing on different rivers. And they continue to be family owned.

As President and Co-Owner of AmaWaterways™, Rudi and his other Co-Owners, Kristin Karst, Executive Vice President, and along with Gary Murphy, Vice-President, Sales, have continue to lead the way with their passion for the river cruising.

Rudi's Suggestions as Far as Being Successful?

The success of AmaWaterways™ has continued on, and when Cindy and Rudi talked about this? Rudi provided a few suggestions. He said, "Take a risk to be successful." And he also said, "Be the best at what you do!"

Rudi truly has taken the river cruise industry to new levels, using his architectural and business expertise. He continues to innovate, and this is best displayed in their beautiful river cruise ships. As Cindy and both have discussed, Rudi truly is the Architect of the River Cruise Industry !

Chapter 10

A Proven Success - Growing Profits AND People... Nicholas Rago, President & CEO, Consultants to Management

Nicholas Rago, President & CEO, Consultants to Management (Photo Courtesy of Nicholas Rago)

An area Cindy and I talk about quite a bit? We discuss how some businesses are successful, while other businesses fail. There is a key area we both agree upon. If a business or corporation is going to be successful, the business needs to continue generating ongoing profits. But they also need to keep focused on the people component – the people, the employees, who work there.

One of the executives Cindy has been fortunate to know for several years, Nicholas Rago, has also focused on this area himself. It is an integral part of his management style and definitely has been a key component of his success leading major corporations over the years.

Since 1998, Nicholas Rago has been President and CEO of Consultants to Management, a Phoenix based firm. Prior to that, throughout his diverse, successful senior management career, Nicholas held top executive positions with several Fortune 100 companies.

A bit more about Nicholas "Nick" Rago? Cindy shared more about him, along with how she first had the pleasure of meeting and getting to know Nick.

Nick was Senior Vice President, Service Companies for DIAL/ VIAD Corporation, a $2.4 billion service company. Nick then became Chairman, President and CEO of Premier Cruise Lines, Ltd. the Official Cruise Line of Walt Disney World™. A role he had from 1993 to 1998, Nick actually negotiated the agreement for Premier Cruise Lines, Ltd. to be the Official Cruise Line of Walt Disney World™. During his time as Chairman, President and CEO of Premier Cruise Lines, Ltd., Nicholas attended and spoke at numerous travel and cruise conferences throughout the USA. This is where Cindy actually had the chance to meet and get to know Nick. And they have continued to keep in touch over the years.

Prior to his role as Chairman, President and CEO of Premier Cruise Lines, Ltd. the official Cruise Line of Walt Disney World™, Nick was Vice President and general manager, Armour Food Company.

Other roles as far as his successful career? Nick served as Senior Vice President and General Manager for the Greyhound Lines. Prior to that, Nick was President of Conagra, Inc. and previous to that,

Nick spent ten years as Director of Marketing for the Campbell Soup Company.

In 1998, Nick decided to take an early retirement from the VIAD Corp, and then founded Consultants to Management. Nick's passion continues, assisting companies grow their profits and people through improving their operations management, sales, marketing, and human resources strategies.

The Important Emphasis on PROFIT and PEOPLE

Sometimes when hearing and reading more about businesses in the world today, it appears the focus tends to be more about their showcasing their ability to make ongoing profits. And many times, also focusing on the people component does not seem to come up as much. Cindy and I both agree that people are also a key part to success.

Nick's success in key roles along with his specialized consulting work emphasizes that a company needs to generate profits, but they also need to focus on the people who make this happen. This is an area that

Nick assists companies with this through Consultants to Management.

As far as the PROFIT and PEOPLE technique? Nick shared more about this with Cindy. He said this particular technique focuses on bringing together all the business units within an organization to effectively perform as an integral partnership.

This results in increased revenue and profit by each employee which then improves efficiency and performance. Nick also mentioned, "You need to get it right the first time." Nick's special training program, "Teambuilding for Team Success" shares more of this.

Bringing that Human Touch In

Nick Rago is definitely a person (or as I like to tell Cindy, a great human) who leads by example. Cindy mentioned that in one of their phone calls, Nick shared some wonderful thoughts, interweaving quotes as well. One he mentioned? He said, "At the end of day, all we have is each other. So, it's especially important to connect with a goal and then connect with a cause as well."

When it comes to history, sometimes people tend to obsess a bit too much on what has taken place – some negative things. But Nick mentioned, "You can't change history. You need to instead learn from history."

As an executive himself who has successfully grown and led different companies in top roles, Nick has always felt that employees are an excellent, extremely valuable source of information. Cindy also saw this as well when she first got to know Nick. At that time, he was Chairman, President and CEO of Premier Cruise Lines, Ltd. Nick and Cindy chatted about this a bit more and he said, "Take time to listen to your employees. This is important."

Nick and Cindy had a discussion about providing compliments. I love compliments myself because they make me feel good and special. Nick shared more thoughts and told Cindy, "It's important to give people compliments. Why? We need to help people succeed. If you give someone a compliment, they will continue to do what you complimented them about. And that helps them succeed."

A Bit More About Nick's "Teambuilding for Team Success"

One of the special trainings Nick has done is his "Teambuilding for Team Success." A high energy training session, Nick focuses on how people, from leaders to followers, can effectively operate as part of a dynamic team.

Nick shared more about this with Cindy. Using Zoom, webinars, videos, and energetic personal interactions, Nick's "Teambuilding for Team Success" encourages people to look inward. This helps them discover how to bring their personal energy and strengths as a joint effort to succeed as part of a company team. In their conversation, Nick also used an analogy about the spoke in a wheel, which is one of the rods that goes from the hub where an axle connects. He said, "Gaining confidence in your role or position to become a strong spoke in the collective wheel is also so important."

Cindy and I both thought this was fascinating. Focusing on being self-motivated to be a catalyst to move forward with personal responsibilities, as well as learning how to use positive communications is another key way you can contribute to a company's success.

Nick's Passion for Helping Companies Achieve their Next Level of Success

Throughout his career, leading companies, and helping them grow combining his model of PROFIT and PEOPLE, Nick has really dedicated his life to helping them also achieve their next level of success. Nick continues to keep on top of industry trends, and he has an acute understanding of the business world. Through his ongoing consulting, along with working directly with small businesses, plus his memberships in several professional organizations, Nick's passion for helping companies achieve their next level of success shows.

Another area where Nick has provided his expertise is with different areas of training and teaching. He has been on the faculty of Maricopa County and Community Colleges. as a marketing and management adjunct instructor. Nick has also been Chairman of the Business and Technical Advisory Board.

Nick candidly says, "I believe in profit and people. When starting in a leadership position at a company, the first thing you need to do is talk to the employees there and harvest them for ideas. Employees know answers and can provide valuable feedback. And these people help you get to the profit part."

Another Area of Nick's Work – Helping Emerging Leaders

For the past 10 years, Nick has been working as the lead instructor for the Emerging Leaders Initiative. This is through the Small Business Administration (SBA) and the Arizona District Office. A bit more about the Emerging Leaders Initiative? This special program features executive-level customized training focusing on improving organizational framework, fostering economic development and sustainability, as well as providing valuable resources including local contacts that increase opportunities for local eligible businesses. Each year 20 businesses are selected as participants.

Helping Companies Their Next Level of Success

Nick's acute understanding of the business world as well as what it takes to be a more successful entity is part of what he continues to bring to the world. And it shows in his continuing dedication helping people achieve their next level of success.

It Is About the People and the Profits

What Nick has shared about the key need to also focus on the people who work at companies, besides their profits is important. Cindy and I both agree that this is what really makes a company successful. The people who work at companies are a true resource as far as understanding how that company runs. And reaching out to them is another part of what it takes to be tremendously successful.

Nicholas Rago, President & CEO, Consultants to Management (Photo courtesy of Nicholas Rago)

Cindy also told me that over the years, Nick has often told her that he is her "Coach." And this continues to mean so much to her as well. As a young lady with four feet instead of two, I do enjoy being around wonderful humans. Cindy and I chat about this. We both love learning more about what a great human does and the part they play in making sure a business is successful. It is a result of focusing on both their people along with making a profit.

Chapter 11
Closing Thoughts

When thinking about what makes a great human, Cindy and I had a good conversation about this. We talked about traits.

While talking and writing about these great humans, some key things came up and we decided to make a list.

Here is our list:

- These humans have a hands-on approach - in my case, a Paws on Approach
- These humans lead by example
- These humans get back to other humans in a very timely way
- These humans focus on the human factor
- These humans also know how to create a fun factor
- These humans continue to grow and learn
- These humans believe in having that personal human interaction, and do not treat others like they are just "worker bees"

- These humans believe in creating their own opportunities that create their own success and "luck"
- They know they CAN create wonderful experiences and opportunities for others

Despite the unexpected challenges that sometimes we see in the world today, it is even more important to focus on positives, building on those true human qualities.

About the Authors – Cindy Bertram & Miss Zooey

Cindy Bertram is a nationally published author, speaker, and well-known storyteller. Her 20+ years of diverse marketing, public relations and branding experience includes areas in the travel and cruise industry. A savvy content creator, marketer and dynamic storyteller, Cindy can take a "blank page" and then through pulling out the true, real stories of a company, their people, and products? She brings that page to life in an incredibly special, unique way. Her diverse writing includes thought leadership pieces, articles, blogs, and industry forecasts. She has also contributed sections to 3 different PR NEWS' Guidebooks. Her passion for giving a helping hand is best seen in her short story, "A Cruise and a Promise," published in *Chicken Soup for the Traveler's Soul.* In her weekly video series, "Extraordinary Not Ordinary," she shares real positive stories. She is also author of *How Six Women Executives Steer the Cruise Industry Today.* Cindy's MBA from Loyola University Chicago works well with her high creative edge and liberal arts B.A

Websites: **www.cindybertram.net & www.bertramedia.net**

https://www.linkedin.com/in/cindybertram

 @cindybertram   CindyBert85

Miss Zooey is very smart, young lady who happens to walk on the floor, with four legs instead of two. She is a great listener, and then will share her thoughts via different methods – not just through barking, but through her energy, whether it be through "moochies" (kisses), using one of her front paws, or through visual eye contact.